LEARNING HOW TO LEARN

Based on the Works of

L. RON HUBBARD

EFFECTIVE
EDUCATION
PUBLISHING

To the Parent or Teacher

Important information about the usage of this book is written on pages 192–194. Familiarity with and application of the data in that section can help your child get more out of the book.

Published by
Effective Education Publishing
11755 Riverview Dr.
St. Louis, MO 63138

Softcover: ISBN 978-1-4031-0278-2

© 1992, 1999
L. Ron Hubbard Library
All Rights Reserved

Contents

CHAPTER ONE:

LEARNING HOW TO LEARN

Learn How to Learn

You can learn anything you want to learn!

Learning is not just getting more and more facts.

A fact is something that is known to be true.

Getting more and more facts is not learning.

Learning is understanding new things and getting better ways to do things.

Before you can learn about something you have to want to learn about that thing.

If you think you know all there is to know about something, you will not be able to learn about it.

The first thing you have to decide is that you want to learn something.

He wants to learn.

She wants to learn.

Do you want to learn?

Once you have decided that there is something you want to learn, the next thing is to study it.

To *study* means to look at something,

and ask about it,

and read about it,

so you learn about it.

Drill

Use a sheet of paper to write down your answer.

What does *learning* mean?

Drill

Use a sheet of paper to write down your answer.

What does *study* mean?

Drill

Use a sheet of paper to write down your answer.

How could you learn to take care of a pet dog?

Drill

Choose something you want to learn about. Use a sheet of paper to write down how you would learn about that thing.

Why You Study

Many people think that they study so they can pass a test.

But that is not what learning is about.

That is not why you study.

You study to *use* what you have learned.

Drill

Use a sheet of paper to write down your answer.

How will you use what you have learned in this section of this book?

Trouble with Study

Some people do not know how to study, so they have trouble learning.

He does not know how to study.

She does not know how to study.

He does not know how to study.

Sometimes you might run into trouble
when you are studying and feel like giving up.

If you understand why you run into trouble and you learn how to get out of trouble, you can study easily.

You can get pretty smart!

This book can help you learn how to learn.

It can teach you how to study.

Drill

Use a sheet of paper to write down your answers.

a. What would you like to learn about?

b. How would it help you to learn about that thing?

Barriers to Study

When you study, you sometimes run into a *barrier* to learning.

A *barrier* is something that blocks the way or stops you from going on.

If you wanted to learn how to sew,

but you had never seen anyone sew,

you might have trouble.

This could be a *barrier* to *study*.

A barrier to study
can make learning hard.

But when you know what the barriers to study are and you can see these barriers and get rid of them, you do not have to be stopped!

You can learn anything you want to learn!

Drill

Use a sheet of paper to write down your answer.

What is a barrier?

CHAPTER TWO:

THE FIRST BARRIER TO STUDY: LACK OF MASS

The First Barrier to Study: Lack of Mass

The first barrier to study is not having the real thing there that you are studying about.

The real things or the objects
that you study about are called *mass*.

If you were studying about cars, you could get the mass of a car by going to a real car and looking at it and touching it.

If you were reading about animals, you could get the mass of animals by going to a zoo or a farm.

Drill

Use a sheet of paper to write down your answer.

How could you get mass if you were studying about cooking?

Studying about something without having the mass of what you are studying can give you trouble.

Studying without the mass of what you are
trying to learn can make you feel squashed,

bent,

sort of spinny,

sort of lifeless,

bored,

or angry.

You can wind up with your stomach feeling funny.

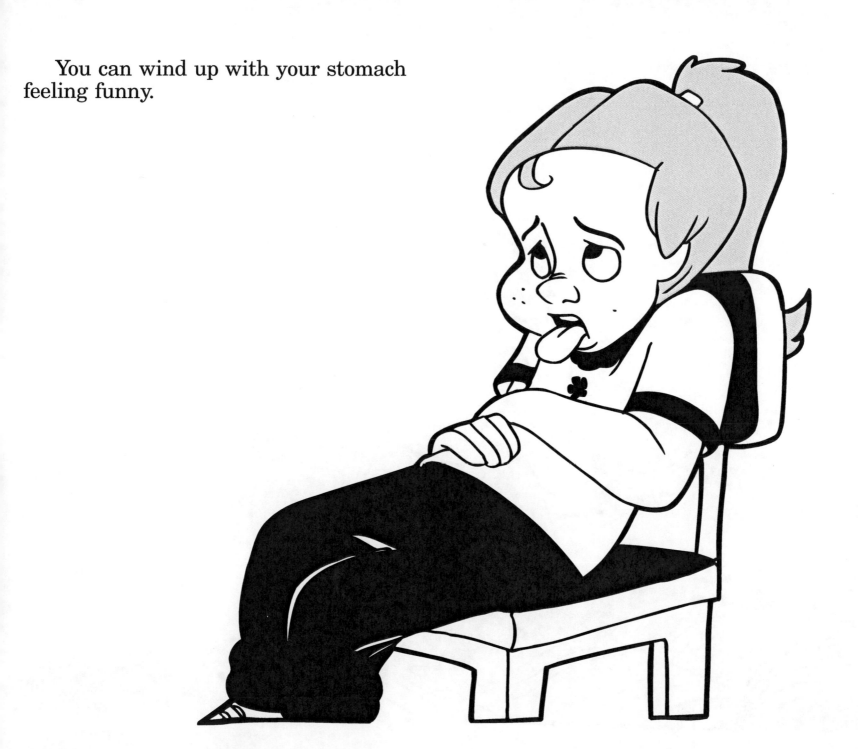

You may get headaches.

You will feel dizzy from time to time

and very often your eyes will hurt.

The way to stop this from happening is to get the mass of what you are studying.

Sometimes you cannot get the real thing
you are studying about.

When you cannot get the real thing, pictures help. Movies would help too.

Reading books or listening to someone talk does not give you mass.

Words and talking do not take the place of what you are studying about.

Drill

Use a sheet of paper to write down your answers.

a. Draw a picture of a person feeling

squashed

bent

spinny

lifeless

bored

angry

b. Why would a student feel these ways?

c. What could you do to help a student who felt these ways?

Drill

Find the mass for each thing listed here and touch it or point to it.

a. water

b. numbers

c. Earth

d. people

e. a light

Drill

Use a sheet of paper to write down your answers.

a. What would you do if you and your brother were in your bedroom and he was explaining to you about the engine in your dad's car and you started to feel bored and your head started to ache?

b. What would you do if your friend was reading a book about how to take care of hamsters but he felt spinny?

CHAPTER THREE:

THE SECOND BARRIER TO STUDY: THE SKIPPED GRADIENT

The Second Barrier to Study: The Skipped Gradient

A gradient is a way of learning or doing something step by step. A gradient can be easy and each step can be done easily.

Or a gradient can be hard and each step is difficult to do.

You learn how to do something by learning to do each part of it step by step.

You go through the first step and learn how to do it.

Then you go to the next step and learn how to do that.

You learn how to do each step well and then you can do the whole thing.

Learning something step by step
is called learning on a gradient.

If you hit a step that seems too hard to do or you feel you can't understand the step you are on, you have skipped a gradient.

"Skipped" means *left out* or *missed*.

If you don't fully understand a step of something you are learning or you miss a step, you will have a skipped gradient.

Skipping a gradient is a barrier to study.

If you have skipped a gradient you may feel a sort of confusion or reeling.

"Reeling" means moving or swaying like you might fall.

An example is a person trying to build something.

He is confused and sort of reeling.

There was too much of a jump because he did not understand what he was doing,

and he jumped to the next thing and that step was too steep.

He will think his trouble is with this new step.

But it is not.

His trouble is at the end of the step he thought he understood well.

Find out what he thought he understood well just before he got all confused.

You will find he did not really understand that step well.

Get this step understood well,

and he will be able to do the next step.

The gradient is no longer skipped.

Drill

Use a sheet of paper to draw a picture of a person who skipped a gradient.

Drill

Use a sheet of paper to write down your answers.

a. Why should you learn new things step by step?

b. What can happen if you do not learn things step by step?

Drill

Use a sheet of paper to write down your answers.

a. Think of a time that you learned something step by step.

b. Draw a picture that shows each step that you did.

Drill

Use a sheet of paper to write down your answer.

You are reading a book but you feel very confused about what you are reading. You are also reeling. What should you do?

CHAPTER FOUR:

THE THIRD AND MOST IMPORTANT BARRIER TO STUDY: THE MISUNDERSTOOD WORD

The Third and Most Important Barrier to Study: The Misunderstood Word

The third and most important barrier to study is the *misunderstood word*.

He has a misunderstood word.

"Mis" means *not* or *wrongly*.

"Misunderstood" means *not understood* or *wrongly understood*.

A misunderstood word is a word which is *not understood,*

or a word which is *wrongly understood.*

She has a misunderstood word.

He has a misunderstood word.

She has a misunderstood word.

She has a misunderstood word.

A misunderstood word
can be a big word

alphabet

or a small word.

him

Have you ever come to the end of a page and realized that you did not remember what you had read?

If you come to the end of a page and do not remember what you have read then there was a word on the page that you did not understand.

Going past a word that you do not understand can make you feel blank,

or tired,

or like you are not there.

You might also feel worried or upset.

These things do not happen only when you are reading.

They can also happen when you hear a word you do not understand.

The only reason a person would stop studying or get confused ideas or not be able to learn is because he has passed a word that he did not understand.

A misunderstood word can make you do wrong things.

A misunderstood word can stop you from doing the things you are studying about.

A misunderstood word can make you want to stop studying.

The way to handle this barrier is to look earlier in what you were reading for a misunderstood word.

WAS THERE A WORD EARLIER THAT YOU DID NOT UNDERSTAND?

Go back to before you got into trouble, and

find the misunderstood word.

Now look that word up in a dictionary.

A dictionary is a word book. A dictionary is used to find the meanings of words, how to say a word, how to spell a word, how to use a word and many other things about words.

Symbols can be misunderstood in the same way that words can be misunderstood.

A symbol is a mark or sign that means something.

Symbols also need to be understood.

The misunderstood word is the most important of the three barriers to study because it is the barrier that can stop you from learning anything at all.

So if you are feeling blank,

or tired,

or not there,

or worried and upset while you are studying,

it is *always*
because of a misunderstood
word or symbol.

Drill

Use a sheet of paper to draw a picture of a person feeling

a. blank

b. tired

c. not there

d. worried and upset

Drill

Use a sheet of paper to write down your answers.

a. Why would a person feel blank or tired or not there while he was studying?

b. If a person felt blank or tired or not there while he was studying, what could you do to help him?

Drill

Use a sheet of paper to write down your answer.

You are reading a book at home. You get to the bottom of the page but you do not remember what the page was about. Why would this happen?

CHAPTER FIVE:

LEARNING THE MEANING OF WORDS

Learning the Meanings of Words

If you are studying and do not feel as bright as you did,

or if you are taking too long on what you are studying,

or you are yawning,

or doodling,

or daydreaming,

you have gone past a misunderstood word.

If you have a misunderstood word, then there are some steps you need to do.

1. Look earlier in your book and find the word you do not understand.

2. Find the word in a dictionary.

3. Look over all of the definitions.

A definition tells you the meaning of a word.

Find the definition that fits what you are reading.

4. Read this definition.

5. Make up sentences using the word that way until you really understand that definition.

You might have to make up many sentences. Maybe ten or more.

That is okay.

The important thing is that you understand what the word means.

6. When you understand the definition that fits in what you were reading, then learn each of the other definitions the same way.

leg ONE OF THE BODY PARTS ON WHICH HUMANS AND ANIMALS SUPPORT THEMSELVES AND WALK.

7. After you learn all of the definitions of that word then go back to what you were reading. If you are not bright and ready to study again, then there is still another word that you do not understand.

Do steps 1-7 again until you are bright and ready to study again.

8. Then start studying from the place where the misunderstood word was.

(If you found more than one misunderstood word, start studying again from the place where you found the earliest misunderstood word.)

More About Learning New Words

Sometimes when words are used together, these words do not mean the same thing as they do all by themselves.

For example, here is a sentence: "The actor's performance will bring the house down." "Bring the house down" means "to receive very loud applause." It does not mean that the actor is going to lower a house using a crane. When words are used like this it is called an *idiom*.

"Bring the house down" does not mean this:

146

"Bring the house down" means this:

I KNEW HIS PERFORMANCE WOULD BRING THE HOUSE DOWN.

Have you ever heard anyone say, "Shake a leg"?

"Shake a leg" does not mean that you should shake your leg.

"Shake a leg" means "to dance."

"Shake a leg" can also mean "to hurry."

Dictionaries show the idioms of a word after the definitions of a word.

leg 1

SHAKE A LEG:
TO DANCE.

If you are learning a word that has idioms you should learn the idioms after the other definitions of the word.

Use the idioms in sentences just like you do when you are learning the other definitions of a word.

When you are learning a word, you may find a word in the definition that you do not understand.

Find that word in the dictionary too, and learn all of its definitions.

Then go back to the first word you were learning.

When you understand all the words in what you are studying you can understand the whole thing.

A MOUSE IS A NICE PET.

THE MOUSE SCARED HER.

MOUSE 1. A SMALL GNAWING ANIMAL THAT LIVES IN HOUSES AND FIELDS.

Drill

Find the word "chicken" in a dictionary. Show another person how you would learn what the word "chicken" means by doing the steps of how to learn the meaning of a word.

Drill

Find a word in something you are studying that you do not know the meaning of. Use a dictionary to find out what that word means using the eight steps of how to learn the meaning of a word.

CHAPTER SIX:

DEMONSTRATION AND LEARNING

Demonstration and Learning

The word "demonstrate" means to show, or to show how something works. A *demonstration* is something done to show something or how it works.

Doing a demonstration is a good way to teach someone something. Demonstration is an important part of learning.

When you are studying, you can do a "demonstration" or "demo" with a "demo kit." A demo kit is made of different objects such as corks, caps, paper clips, pen tops, rubber bands or other similar objects. You can demonstrate an idea or rule or anything you are studying with your hands and the pieces of your demo kit.

This is a demo kit.

If you ran into something you could not figure out, a demo kit would help you to understand it. You can make different pieces of the demo kit take the place of the things you are studying about. You can move the objects around to see how something works.

By doing this you get mass that helps you understand the ideas you are studying about.

Drill

Make a demo kit for yourself.

Drill

Using your demo kit, show another person how you would get from home to school.

Drill

Using your demo kit, demo the first barrier to study to another person.

Demo how you would help someone who has the first barrier to study.

Drill

Using your demo kit, demo the second barrier to study to another person.

Demo how you would help someone who has the second barrier to study.

Drill

Using your demo kit, demo the third barrier to study to another person.

Demo how you would help someone who has the third barrier to study.

Drill

Use a sheet of paper to write down your answer.

Why would you do a demo when you are studying?

Clay Demonstration

Another way to demonstrate what you are studying is to make it in clay. This is called a "clay demonstration" or "clay demo." Demonstrating something in clay can help you to figure out how something is put together, how it looks or how it works. It can help you understand better what you are studying.

If you come across something you cannot figure out, you can work it out in clay.

There are many ways that clay can be used.

People who design new cars make clay models of cars to see how they will look.

A general will make a model of the battle-field so he can get an idea of how to win the battle.

You can understand *anything* better by demonstrating it in clay. Say you wanted to figure out how to organize your room better so you could fit a new desk in it. You could make a model of the room and the furniture and other things. Then you could move them around and find the best way to arrange them.

How to Do a Clay Demo

Clay demos are done using clay to make the mass of the thing. Then a label is made to say what the thing is. Let's see how this works.

If you want to do a clay demo of a pencil, first make a thin roll of clay. This is the pencil lead. Then make a label that says "LEAD" and stick it on the thin roll of clay.

Next, put another layer of clay with the thin roll sticking out a little bit at one end. This is the wood part of the pencil, so make a label that says "WOOD" and stick it on.

Then put another little piece of clay on the end. This is the rubber eraser, so label it "RUBBER" and stick it on that piece of clay.

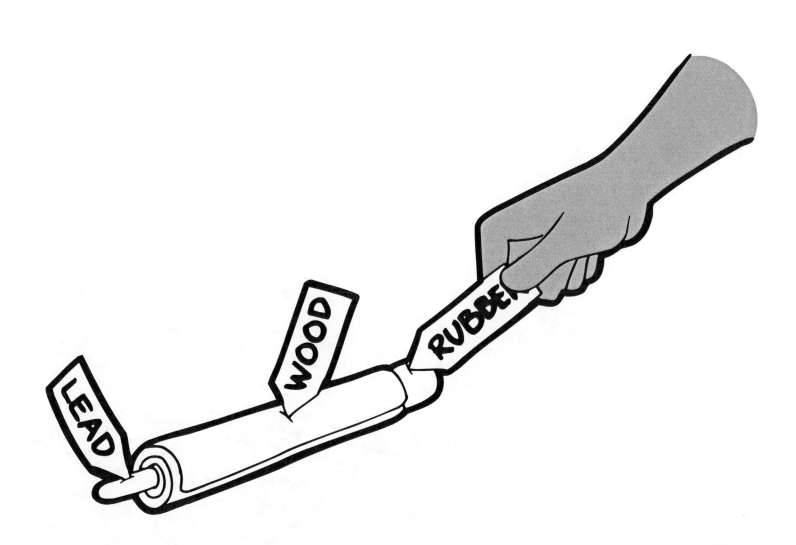

Finally, you make a label for the whole thing. This label says "PENCIL."

Clay demos must be large. If a clay demo is too small it might not make what you are studying real enough. Making the things you are studying in clay can help make them more *real* to you.

Her clay demo is large.

Her clay demo is too small.

Making BIG clay demos works better to help you understand what you are studying.

Even a thought can be shown in clay: You can use a thin ring of clay to show a thought or idea. Here is a clay demo of a person thinking about a ball.

If you don't understand something in life you can work it out in clay and understand it better. *Anything* can be shown in clay.

Clay demos are an important part of learning how to learn.

Sketching

A sketch is a rough drawing of something.

Sketching is also a part of demonstration and part of working things out.

You sometimes see people doing sketching at work. They work things out for themselves by sketching it.

Drill

Do a sketch of how to get from your house to your friend's house.

Summary

People who do well in life never really stop studying and learning.

There are a lot of things to learn.

Learning is not hard to do and it can be fun.

Now that you know the barriers to study and how to handle them, you can learn anything you want to learn.

And you can help others learn too!

WE ARE GOING TO FIND THE WORD YOU DO NOT UNDERSTAND.

Drill

Use a sheet of paper to write down your answer.

Why will it help you to know how to study?

Drill

Get a short, simple book about something you are interested in learning.

Read the book. If you run into any of the barriers to study while you are reading, then use what you have learned in this book to handle the barriers.

Use a sheet of paper to write down what you did.

CONGRATULATIONS!

You have completed *Learning How to Learn.*

Knowing how to learn is useful and important. It is very well done that you have learned this.

Have fun using your new skills to learn anything you want to learn. That is what they are for!

Important Information for Parents and Teachers

This book has been published to fill an important need.

We live now in an instruction-book world. Our civilization is highly technical.

Formal education today goes into one's twenties, nearly a third of a lifetime. But what happens when a person leaves school? Can he *do* what he studied? And factually, education begins *before* a person learns to speak and continues throughout his entire life. Can he *do* what he has studied outside of the classrooms of his school days?

Any child's future success and happiness are dependent on his ability to learn. Innately, this ability is very strong. Children possess an almost boundless fascination about everything in life. A curiosity and eagerness to explore and learn is turned on "high" at a very young age.

Children are confronted with so many things they don't yet understand. They have been told that learning is the key to their future. But it is a mean trick to tell someone that he must learn and then not teach him HOW to learn.

Learning How to Learn contains fundamental principles of L. Ron Hubbard's researches into the field of education, where he isolated the basics which underlie all forms of learning. His breakthroughs resulted in Study Technology, the first subject which actually deals with HOW to learn. Study Technology is basic to any specific subject since it deals with learning itself, the barriers to learning and remedies for these barriers.

Learning How to Learn presents the fundamentals of Study Technology at a level that a child can assimilate, understand and use. It is a breakthrough in the field of learning and education for preteenagers and teenagers.

Using the Book for Maximum Benefit

Reading Level

The book is written so that a child can study it by himself It has been written for children eight through twelve, though children as young as six have successfully read the book, grasped the concepts and put them to use.

Drills

There are drills throughout the book which get the child to apply what he has read. These are key to gaining the most from the book and the child should be encouraged to do them thoroughly.

Familiarity

In working with a son or daughter on the book or in using it in a classroom, it will help if you have read the book first and are familiar with its contents. Though simply written, the data presented here are not to be found in any previously published book on education or learning. The concepts are totally original with the researches of L. Ron Hubbard into the field of education and his discoveries on the mental phenomena which block learning, the physiological manifestations which result from these blocks and the specific remedies for each one.

Ensuring Understanding

In giving this book to your son or daughter and in working with him or her on the book or in using it in a classroom situation, there is one very important datum about study of which you should be aware:

THE ONLY REASON A PERSON GIVES UP A STUDY OR BECOMES CONFUSED OR UNABLE TO LEARN IS BECAUSE HE HAS GONE PAST A WORD THAT WAS NOT UNDERSTOOD.

The confusion or inability to grasp or learn comes AFTER a word that the person did not have defined and understood.

Have you ever had the experience of coming to the end of a page and realizing you didn't know what you had read? Well, somewhere earlier on that page you went past a word that you had no definition for or an incorrect definition for.

Here's an example. "It was found that when the crepuscule arrived the children were quieter and when it was not present, they were livelier." You see what happens. You think you don't understand the whole idea, but the inability to understand came entirely from the one word you could not define, *crepuscule*, which means twilight or darkness.

The datum about not going past an undefined word is the most important datum in study and is thoroughly covered in the book on pages 101–127. Every subject a person has taken up and then abandoned or done poorly at had its words which the person failed to get defined. It is the most important barrier to study and a parent or teacher should be familiar with this datum. The phenomena which occur after a person has unknowingly encountered a word he or she did not understand are quite distinct and easily recognized once you know what you are looking at.

As simple as it seems, many of the tribulations in children's lives can often be traced back to words they have not understood in their reading materials or in life.

Use As a Reference Book

After a child has read the book and learned these study skills, he can and should be referred back to his materials whenever necessary during his future studies. As startling as it may seem, a workable technology of how to study something was foreign to the field of education before L. Ron Hubbard's researches in the area. *Learning How to Learn* can be used time and time again as a reminder of the basics of successful learning.

Further Information

Numerous schools across the United States and throughout Europe now utilize Mr. Hubbard's Study Technology to promote faster learning with increased comprehension.

If you or your child or student encounter any difficulties in reading or applying the data in this book there are addresses of schools and institutions on the following pages you can contact. These organizations make exclusive use of Study Technology and will be happy to provide any assistance needed as well as provide further information about these new advances in education.

For further information contact:
Applied Scholastics International
Phone: (314) 355-6355 – Fax: (314) 355-2621
E-mail: education@appliedscholastics.org
Website: www.appliedscholastics.org.

——————

When a child knows how to gain more knowledge, his enthusiasm for learning will never become stale. The basic concepts presented in this book apply to anyone, not just children. Once a child grasps the tools contained here these will become a natural part of his approach to living and he will use them throughout all his activities in life.

The fundamentals contained in *Learning How to Learn* are sweeping discoveries in the field of education and they open the gates to learning and application.

When a child has learned how to learn, all knowledge becomes available to him, assuring that, whatever his fields of interest, he will have the greatest possible chance for fulfillment and success.

About the Author

L. Ron Hubbard was no stranger to education. Although his main profession was that of a professional writer, in a long, event-filled and productive life he spent thousands of hours researching in the education field, lecturing and teaching.

He was born in Tilden, Nebraska on 13 March 1911, and his early years were spent on his grandfather's ranch in the wilds of Montana. As the son of a US Navy commander, he was well on the way to becoming a seasoned traveler by the age of eight, and by the time he was nineteen he had logged over a quarter of a million miles.

He enrolled in George Washington University in 1930, taking classes in mathematics and engineering. But his was not a quiet academic life. He took up flying in the pioneer days of aviation, learning to pilot first glider planes and then powered aircraft. He worked as a freelance reporter and photographer. He directed expeditions to the Caribbean and Puerto Rico, and later, to Alaska. The world was his classroom and he studied voraciously, gathering experience which provided the background for his later writings, research and discoveries.

Some of his first published articles were nonfiction, based upon his aviation experience. Soon he began to draw from his travels to produce a wide variety of fiction stories and novels: adventure, mystery, westerns, fantasy and science fiction.

The proceeds from his fiction writing funded his main line of research and exploration-how to improve the human condition. His nonfiction works cover such diverse subjects as drug rehabilitation, marriage and family, success at work, statistical analysis, public relations, art, marketing and much, much more. But he did more than write books—he also delivered over 3,000 lectures and conducted courses to impart his own discoveries to others.

However, in order to learn, one must be able to read and understand. Therefore, L. Ron Hubbard tackled the problem of teaching others how to study. His research uncovered the basic reason for the failure of a student to grasp any subject. He discovered the barriers to full comprehension of what one is studying, and developed methods by which anyone can improve his ability to learn and to *apply* the data that he is being taught. He wrote a considerable body of work on this subject, which he termed *Study Technology*.

L. Ron Hubbard's advanced technology of study is now used by an estimated two million students and thousands of teachers in universities and school systems internationally. His educational materials have been translated into more than eighteen languages to meet this worldwide demand for the first truly workable technology of how to study. Oranizations delivering L. Ron Hubbard's Study Technology have been established in many countries including the United States, Australia, South Africa, Canada, Austria, Great Britain, Mexico, Germany, Denmark, France, Italy, Venezuela and Taiwan.

L. Ron Hubbard departed this life on 24 January 1986. His contributions to the world of education have meant new hope, better understanding and increased ability for millions of students and educators the world over.

L. RON HUBBARD

Additional Books for Students by L. Ron Hubbard

Study Skills for Life • Written for preteens and young teenagers, this book teaches students how to *use* what they are studying so they can attain the goals they set for themselves. Using these skills, they can break the barriers to learning.

How to Use a Dictionary Picture Book for Children • One of the ingredients of a quality education is giving a student the tools he needs to study successfully on his own. No matter the subject or field being learned, one has to know how to use the dictionary to clearly understand the meaning of words. This book contains the secret of how to put education into action.

Grammar and Communication • The ability to communicate is vital to happiness and self-confidence. But getting one's communication across is dependent upon being able to speak and write correctly. The unique approach to grammar taught in this book can open the world of words to a child-granting him the strong sense of self-esteem which results from the ability to read well, write clearly and communicate effectively.

When children can learn and think for themselves, the world is an open book.

TO ORDER THESE BOOKS OR TO GET MORE INFORMATION ON L. RON HUBBARD'S STUDY TECHNOLOGY, CONTACT:

Applied Scholastics International
11755 River View Drive
St. Louis, Missouri 63138, USA
Phone: (314) 355-6355
Fax: (314) 355-2621
E-mail: education@appliedscholastics.org
Website: www.appliedscholastics.org

For more information on educational books and materials by L. Ron Hubbard, contact your nearest distributor:

Applied Scholastics International
11755 River View Drive
St. Louis, Missouri 63138

United States of America

Applied Scholastics Eastern United States
1 Red Mill Lane
Darien, Connecticut 06820

Applied Scholastics Western United States
7060 Hollywood Blvd., Suite 320
Los Angeles, California 90028

Canada

Applied Scholastics Canada
1680 Lakeshore Road West, Unit 5A
Mississauga, Ontario
Canada L5J lJ4

United Kingdom

Applied Scholastics UK
Coombe Hall, Coombe Hall Road
East Grinstead, W. Sussex
England

Europe

Applied Scholastics Europe
F.F. Ulriksgade 13
2100 Copenhagen Ø
Denmark

South Africa

Education Alive South Africa
3rd Floor CDH House
217 Jeppe Street
Johannesburg 2001
South Africa

Australia

Applied Scholastics Australia,
   New Zealand, Oceania
89-97 Jones Street, 4th Floor, Suite 64
Ultimo, NSW 2007
Australia

You can also contact any of the groups and organizations on the following pages which use L. Ron Hubbard's study technology.

Applied Scholastics Groups and Organizations

United States of America

California

Applied Scholastics Outreach
P.O. Box 29726
Los Angeles, California 90029

Ability Plus School
Orange County
220 El Canulno Real
Thstin, California 92780

Advanced Education Technologies, Inc.
8727 Fenwick
Sunland, California 91040

Aptos Academy
181 Ridgeview Drive
Aptos, California 95003

Bradberry Institute
11120 Oro Vista Avenue
Sunland, California 91040

Brighten School
1102 N. Granada Drive
Orange, California 92869

California Ranch School
17305 Santa Rosa Mine Road
Penis, California 92570-9540

Canyon View Academy
8100 McGroarty Street
Sunland, California 91040

Carroll-Roes Academy
4474 De Longpre
Los Angeles, California 90027

CLIC Pacoima
9650 Saluda Avenue
Tujunga, California 91042

Delphi Academy Los Angeles
4490 Cornishon Avenue
La Canada, California 91011

Delphi Academy Sacramento
5590 Madison Avenue
Sacramento, California 95841

Delphi Academy San Diego
3401 Clairmont Drive
San Diego, California 92117

Delphi Academy San Francisco
890 Palinoroy Avenue #201
Santa Clara, California 95051

Effective Training Solutions
39355 California Street #207
Fremont, California 94538

Expansion Consultants
2609 Honolulu Avenue,
Suite 203
Montrose, California 91020

Golden Gate Apple School
379 Colusa Avenue
Kensington, California 94707

HELP Orange County
5 Capstone Road
Irvine, California 92606

HELP Tutor Training Academy
4490 Cornishon Avenue
La Canada, California 91011

Hollywood Education & Literacy Project
6336 Hollywood Blvd.
Hollywood, California 90028

Learning Connection
2528 Canyon Drive
Hollywood, California 90068

Learning Plus
220 Belgatos Road
Los Gatos, California 95032

Los Gatos Academy
220 Belgatos Road
Los Gatos, California 95032

Mary's School House
1334 L. Ron Hubbard Way
Los Angeles, California 90027

Mojave Desert School
44579 Temescal
Newberry Springs, California 92365

Pinewood Academy
4490 Cornishon Avenue
La Canada, California 91011

Professional Tutoring Services
4453 Utah Street
San Diego, California 92116

Ranchito Tutoring School
6945 Ranchito Avenue
Van Nuys, California 91405

Renaissance Academy La Canada
4490 Corishon Avenue
La Canada, California 91011

Sonoma Valley Academy
276 East Napa Street
Sonoma, California 95476

Superphonics Tutoring
39833 90th Street West
Leona Valley, California 93551

Taplin Corporate Training
127W. Lanes Road
Thousand Oaks, California 91360

World Literacy Crusade
3209 N. Alameda, Suite B
Compton, California 90262

World Literacy Crusade Sacramento
9647 Folsom Blvd. #350
Sacramento, California 95827

Colorado

Ability Plus School Colorado
3375 5. Bannock, Suite 101
Englewood, Colorado 80110

Literacy for Life, Inc.
3375 5. Bannock, Suite 220
Englewood, Colorado 80110

Connecticut

Standard Education
68 Prospect Street
Waterbury, Connecticut 06702

Florida

Applied Scholastics Florida
1158 Brook Drive
Clearwater, Florida 34615

A Star Academy
P.O. Box 4351
Clearwater, Florida 33756

Back to Basics School
253 Grove Circle South
Dunedin, Florida 34698

Better Learning Center
1774 Pineland Drive
Clearwater, Florida 33755

Bowens Enterprises
9929 East Regency Row
Inverness, Florida 34450

Clearwater Academy International
801 Drew Street
Clearwater, Florida 33755-4517

Conway Academy
P.O. Box 533993
Orlando, Florida 32853-3993

Delphi Academy Florida
1831 Drew Street
Clearwater; Florida 34625

HELP Miami
7867 NW 52nd
Miami, Florida 33166

Applied Scholastics Florida
1158 Brook Drive
Clearwater; Florida 34615

Little School
217 Kerry Drive
Clearwatei; Florida 33758

Live Oak Academy
1533 Long Street
Clearwater; Florida 33755

Payson Girl's Choice
P.O. Box 161
Clearwater; Florida 34617

Shady Lane School
3765 Goldsmith Road
Brooksville, Florida, 34602

Smart Apple Tutoring
306 N. Osceola Avenue
Clearwater, Florida 33755

Studema Clearwater
P.O. Box 981
Clearwater; Florida 34617

Vassallo Academy
5741 SW 45 Terrace
Miami, Florida 33155

Welch Study Technology Center
2285 Sharkey Road
Clearwater, Florida 33765

World Literacy Crusade of Florida
1405 NW 167th#235
Miami, Florida 33169

World Literacy Crusade of Pinellas
County
1611 N. Fort Harrison Avenue
Clearwater; Florida 33755

Georgia

Harambee Learning Connection
1215 Ashley Place
Stone Mountain, Georgia 30083

Lafayette Academy
2417 Canton Road
Marietta, Georgia 30066

Hawaii

Applied Scholastics Hawaii
94-348 Hokuala Street #120
Mililani Town, Hawaii 96789-2319

Illinois

Applied Scholastics Chicago
3824W. 147th Street
Midlothian, Illinois 60445

Chicagoland
9 Walnut Road
Glen Ellyn, Illinois 60137

Louisiana

HELP Baton Rouge
P.O. Box 78168
Baton Rouge, Louisiana 70838

Maryland

Woods Tutoring Center
3901 Thoroughbred Lane
Owings Mills, Maryland 21117

Massachusetts

Boston Academy
33 Pearl Street
Somerville, Massachusetts 02145

Delphi Academy Boston
564 Blue Hill Avenue
Milton, Massachusetts 02186

HELP Boston
74 Dix Street #3
Dorchester, Massachusetts 02122

Michigan

Recording Institute of Detroit
14611 E. Nine Mile Road
East Detroit, Michigan 48021

Missouri

Ability School St. Louis
10264 Chaucer Avenue
St. Louis, Missouri 63114

Nevada

Mission of the Children
1018E. Sahara#D
Las Vegas, Nevada 89104

World Literacy Crusade Las Vegas
4738 Yuma Avenue
Las Vegas, Nevada 89104

New Hampshire

Bear Hill School, Inc.
P.O. Box 4l7
Pittsfield, New Hampshire 03263

New Jersey

Ability School New Jersey
192 W. Demarest Avenue
Englewood, New Jersey 07631

CMI Haitian Community Center
P.O. Box l63
Elizabeth, New Jersey 07207

HELP Elizabeth New Jersey
465 Broad Street
Elizabeth, New Jersey 07208

Westcott Study Technology Center
310 O'Donnell Lane
Cinnaminson, New Jersey 08077

New York

Brooklyn World Literacy Crusade
905 Winthrop Street R. 120
Brooklyn, New York 11203

Harlem Literacy Project
259W. 123 Street
New York, New York 10027

New Generation Tutoring Center
4963 Broadway
New York, New York 10034

Ohio

World Literacy Crusade Columbus
101 W. Dunedin Road
Columbus, Ohio 43214

Oregon

Columbia Academy
9806 SW Boones Ferry Road
Portland, Oregon 97219

HELP Portland
5715 NE Sacramento #10
Portland, Oregon 97213

The Delphian School Oregon
20950 SW Rock Creek Road
Sheridan, Oregon 97378

Pennsylvania

Applied Scholastics Pennsylvania
P.O. Box 662
Reading, Pennsylvania 19603

Texas

Applied Scholastics Texas
5110 San Felipe, 136W.
Houston, Texas 77056

Applied Scholastics Houston
2310 River Valley
Missouri City, Texas 77489

Tanglewood Academy
5714 Dolores Street
Houston, Texas 77057

World Literacy Crusade Houston
2310 River Valley
Missouri City, Texas 77489

Utah

Ability School Utah
913 E. Syrena Circle
Sandy, Utah 89094

Virginia

Chesapeake Ability School
5533 Industrial Drive
Springfield, Virginia 22151

Puerto Rico

HELP Puerto Rico
HCO1Box8844
Canóvanas, Puerto Rico 00729

Canada

Academie Phenix
707 rue Jarry East
Montreal, Quebec, Canada H2P 1W3

Education Alive Halifax
2130 Armcrescent West
Halifax, Nova Scotia, Canada B3L 3E3

Education Alive Kentville
27 James Street
Kentville, Nova Scotia, Canada B4N 2A1

Education Alive Toronto
25 Roblin Avenue
East York, Ontario, Canada M4C 3T7

Heritage School
8610 Ash Street
Vancouver, BC, Canada V6P 3M2

Ottawa Literacy Program
1342 Bethamy Lane
Gloucester, Ontario, Canada K1J 8P4

Petit Phenix
707 rue Jarry East
Montreal, Quebec, Canada H2P 1W3

Privileged Academics
62 Calverly Trail
Scarborough, Ontario, Canada MiC 3R5

Progressive Academy
12245-131 Street
Edmonton, Alberta, Canada TSL 1M8

Toronto Ability School
1146 Clarkson Road North
Mississauga, Ontario, Canada LSJ 2W2

West Coast Tutoring
1437 Clyde Avenue
West Vancouver, BC, Canada V7T 1E9

Latin America

Applied Scholastics Mexico
Apdo. Postal 85-061
Mexico, D.F. 10201, Mexico

Buenos Aires Freedom
Moldes 2727
1428 Capital Federal, Buenos Aires
Argentina

Campaña mexicana para mejorar
el estudio
Apdo. Postal 85-061
Mexico, D.F. 10201, Mexico

Educación del Mafiana
Minerva, 395
Colonia Florida
Mexico, D.F. 01030, Mexico

Educación Efectiva Venezuela
Avenida Martin Tovar cruce
con Rondón
Edit Piedra E Tranca, Piso 1 of 101
Valencia, Venezuela

Institute Logos
P.O. Box 2243 2100
Costa Rica
Central America

ITE de Guadalajara
Jazmin, 376 S.R.
Guadalajara, Jalisco, Mexico

ITE de Jalapa
Corregidora, #24-A, Col. Centro
Jalapa, Veracruz
Mexico, D.F. 91000, Mexico

United Kingdom

Achievement Unlimited
6 Smorlets
East Grinstead, Sussex RH19 1TJ
England

Education Excellence
12 Wouldham Road
London E16 lES, England

Effective Education Scotland
14 Esslemont Road
Edinburgh EH16 SPX, Scotland

Effective Education UK
Coombe Hall, Coombe Hall Road
East Grinstead, W. Sussex
England

Greenfields Saturday School
2a The Curve
London 5W12 0RH, England

Greenfields School London
2a The Curve
London 5W12 0RH, England

Greenfields School
Priory Road, Forest Row
East Sussex RH19 5JD, England

Tutoring Centre
30 North Court Road
Worthing, West Sussex BN14 7DR
England

Austria

Kreativ College
Rienosslgasse 12
1040 Wien, Austria

Czech Republic

LITE Anglicka Skola Praha
Kladska 7
12000 Praha 2, Czech Republic

Denmark

Applied Scholastics Denmark
F.F. Ulriksgade 13
2100 Copenhagen Ø., Denmark

Amager International School
Engvej 141-145
2300 Copenhagen S., Denmark

FEGU Aalborg
Lemvigvej 91
Nr. Tranners
9220 Aalborg, Denmark

FEGU Amager
Engvej 141
2300 Copenhagen S., Denmark

FEGU Århus
Hammervamget 22
8310 Tranbjerg
Århus, Denmark

FEGU Arhus N.
Nordre Ringgade 108, 2
8200 Århus N., Denmark

FEGU Birker0d
Kongevejen 110 B
3460 Birkerød, Denmark

FEGU Bjerge
Skolelodden 4
4480 St. Fuglede, Denmark

FEGU Brøndby Strand
Hyttebovej 20
2660 Brøndby Strand, Denmark

FEGU Brønshøj
Klintevej 40
2700 Brønshøj, Denmark

FEGU Ebeltoft
Dragsmurvej 16
8420 Knebel, Denmark

FEGU Egaa
Vesttoften 7
8250 Egaa, Denmark

FEGU Frederiksberg
Philip Schousvej 21 st.
2000 Frederiksberg, Denmark

FEGU Glostrup
Falkevej 20
2600 Glostrup, Denmark

FEGU Grindsted
Grønlandsvej 2
7200 Grindsted, Denmark

FEGU Holte
Carlsmindevej 24
Søllerød, 2840 Holte
Denmark

FEGU Kalundborg
Dalsvinget 5
4400 Kalundborg, Denmark

FEGU Kerteminde
Præstegade 72
5300 Kerteminde, Denmark

FEGU Kjellerup
Blichersvej 28
8620 Kjellerup, Denmark

FEGU Køge
Strædet 6
Strøby Egede
4600 Køge, Denmark

FEGU Næstved
Ndr. Farimagsvej 2
4700 Næstved, Denmark

FEGU Nørrebro
Ravnsborggade 6,5
2200 Copenhagen N., Denmark

FEGU Nørre Sundby
Jørgen Bertelsensvej 17A
9400 Nørres Sundby, Denmark

FEGU Nykøbing F.
Banegårdspladsen 9
4800 Nykøbing F., Denmark

FEGU Odense
Købkesvej 48
5230 Odense, Denmark

FEGU Ølstykke
Safirsvej 21
3650 Ølstykke, Denmark

FEGU Østerbro
F.F. Ulriksgade 13
2100 Copenhagen Ø., Denmark

FEGU Renders
Østergade 16
8900 Randers, Denmark

FEGU Slagelse
Sct. Mikkelsgade 23
4200 Slagelse, Denmark

FEGU Vanløse
Alekistevej 221
2720 Vanløse, Denmark

FEGU Vejle
Hans Egedesvej 7
Vinding
7100 Vejle, Denmark

Kildeskolen
Roskildevej 158
2S00 Valby, Denmark

Kildeskolen Arhus
Klamsagervej 6
8230 Abyhøj, Denmark

Sønderjyllands International Skole
Visgårdsvej 2
Bjerndrup
6200 Abenrå, Denmark

France

Institut Aubert
62, avenue de Paris
94300 Vincennes, France

Management Distribution
31, rue Bressigny
49100 Angers, France

Hungary

Applied Scholastics Hungary
1077 Budapest
Almassy Ter 16. 1/12, Hungary

Ability School Hungary
8142 Urhida
Dozsa Gyorgy u. 6, Hungary

Israel

ATID
Hmagil 2 Street
Tel Aviv, Israel

Yeholet Consulting & Guidance
P.O. Box 37020
Tel Aviv, Israel

Italy

Applied Scholastics Italy
Via B. Melzi, 43
20027 Rescaldina, Milan, Italy

ANCIM
Piazza S. Lucia
00060 Castelnuovo di Porto
Roma, Italy

Associazione Brescia
Via Tese, 46
25020 Capriano del Colle, Italy

OASI School
Via Marco Polo, 5
22063 Cantii (Como), Italy

Netherlands

Applied Scholastics Holland
Fahrenheitstraat 99
1097 Amsterdam, Netherlands

Lafayette School
Fahrenheitstraat 99
1097 Amsterdam, Netherlands

Study Centre M.E.O. Amsterdam
Fabrenheitstraat 99
1097 Amsterdam, Netherlands

Sweden

Applied Scholastics Sweden
12432 Bandhagen
Kallforsvågen 40, Sweden

Barbro Roos Community Services
Box 7S32
200 42 Malmö, Sweden

Daghenimet Måsen
121 33 Eskedalen
Tappgrönd 10-12, Sweden

Daghemmet U-Care
121 33 Eskedalen
Tappgrönd 10, Sweden

Fritidshemmet Robin Hood
12432 Bandhagen
Kållforsvägen 40, Sweden

Studema-skolan
12432 Bandhagen
Källforsvägen 40, Sweden

Switzerland

Mont Savoir
Victor Ruffy 79
1012 Lausanne, Switzerland

Verein ZIEL
Luegetenstrasse 23
6102 Malters, Switzerland

ZIEL Tutoring
Badenerstrasse 294
8004 Zurich, Switzerland

*Commonwealth of
Independent States*

Applied Scholastics Russia
129301 Moscow
Borisa Galushkina Str. 19A
Russia

Applied Scholastics Nizhny Novgorod 1
603158 Nizhny Novgorod
Zaitseva Str. 3, Apt 30
Russia

Applied Scholastics Nizhny Novgorod 2
603032 Nizhny Novgorod
Architekturnaja Str. 9, Apt 11
Russia

Applied Scholastics Taldykorgan
Kazatlistan
P.O. Box 25, Taldykorgan

Education Center Siberia
Usolye-Sibirskoye
Kuibysheva Str. la, Irkutsk Region
Russia

School Ekstern
191014 St. Petersburg
Nekrasova Str. 17/19
Russia

Studema Ekaterinburg
620033 Ekaterinburg
Papanina Str. #9
Russia

Studema Kemerovo
650002 Kemerovo
Institutskaya Str. 28-123
Russia

Africa

Bushbuckridge
P.O. Box 70406
Bryanston
South Africa

Education Alive School
3rd Floor CDH House, 217 Jeppe Street
Johannesburg 2001
South Africa

Education Alive Johannesburg
3rd Floor CDH House, 217 Jeppe Street
Johannesburg 2001
South Africa

Education Alive Cape Town
51 Station Road, Observatory
Cape Town 7925
South Africa

Fairfields Academy
c/o St. Francis Catholic Church
P.O. Box 6, Dompin-Pepesa
Via Tarkwa, W/R Ghana

West Africa

Helping Hands
BlO Villa Alto Douro, Berg St. Belgrav
Johannesburg 2094
South Africa

Summerhill Preparatory School
P.O. Box 2465
Halfway House 1685
South Africa

Australia

Applied Scholastics Darwin
P.O. Box 1536
Humpty Doo 0836
Northern Territory

Australia

Applied Scholastics Training Centre
89-97 Jones Street, 4th Floor, Suite 64
Ultimo, NSW 2007
Australia

Applied Scholastics Victoria
P.O. Box 540
Box Hill, Victoria 3128
Australia

Applied Scholastics Wollongong
P.O. Box 21
Corrimal, NSW 2518
Australia

Athena School
Suite 6, 44 Smith Street
Balmain, NSW 2041
Australia

Braddon Literacy Group
65 Lotanna Street
Braddon, ACT 2601
Australia

Canberra Learning Program
3/32 Sid Barnes Cres, Gordon 2900
Canberra, ACT
Australia

Education Made Easy
6/54 Kneen Street
North Fitzroy, Victoria 3068
Australia

Future Track
7 Dalray Place
Lilydale, Victoria 3140
Australia

Sean Holbrook Community Services
6 Camillo Street
Pendle Hill, NSW 2145
Australia

Street School Blacktown
3 Horns Avenue
Gymea Bay, NSW 2227
Australia

Street School Redfern
34 Edith Street
Bardwell Park, NSW 2207
Australia

Wollongong Learning Program
2 Ziems Place
Towradgi, NSW 2518
Australia

Yarralinda School
4 Birchwood Drive
Mooroolbark, Victoria 3138
Australia

Indonesia

Singgih Tutoring Services
JL Argopuro No. 34
Surabaya, Indonesia

Japan

Applied Scholastics Japan
8-18 Higashi Hakushima
Naka-ku, Hiroshima
Japan 730

Malaysia

Applied Scholastics Malaysia
No. 42-2A Jalan Tun Sambanthan 3
50470 Kuala Lumpur
Malaysia

New Zealand

Henderson High School
8 Hopetown Street
Ponsonby, Auckland
New Zealand

OTARA
2/151 Orlando Drive
Manakau City
New Zealand

Speak Better English
8 Seddon Avenue
Papatoetoe, Auckland
New Zealand

Taiwan

Applied Scholastics Taiwan
87, No. 6 Lane 75 Sec. 4, Nan-king E. Road
Taipei, Taiwan